apprentice
walking the way of christ

Other Books by Steve Chalke

Change Agents: 25 Hard Lessons in the Art of Getting Things Done

Intelligent Church: A Journey Towards Christ-Centred Community (with Anthony Watkis)

The Lost Message of Jesus (with Alan Mann)

apprentice
walking the way of Christ

5 SESSIONS

STEVE CHALKE
and JOANNA WYLD

ZONDERVAN®

ZONDERVAN.com/
AUTHORTRACKER
follow your favorite authors

ZONDERVAN

Apprentice Participant's Guide
Copyright © 2009 by Steve Chalke

Requests for information should be addressed to:

Zondervan, *Grand Rapids, Michigan 49530*

ISBN 978-0-310-32234-4

Cover and interior design by Ben Fetterley

Printed in the United States of America

09 10 11 12 13 14 15 16 17 18 • 23 22 21 20 19 18 17 16 15 14 13 12 11 10 9 8 7 6 5 4 3 2

CONTENTS

JOURNEYING

Who is it that can tell me who I am?

William Shakespeare, *King Lear*

DVD SEGMENT 1

Watch the first video clip for session 1, in which Steve Chalke describes Jesus the rabbi and introduces us to the idea that we are apprentices of Christ. Steve also explores the idea that life is a journey, a quest for identity. If we choose to follow Jesus on our journey, we become his apprentices. Being an apprentice means embracing an active and communal learning style, based on relationship, experience, struggle, mistakes, debate and practice.

With each video clip throughout the participant's guide, space for note-taking is provided.

DVD Notes

'Follow me ...' (Mark 10:21; Luke 14:27; John 12:26)

Disciples as apprentices

Learning together through debate, practice and mistakes

The Bible was written for communities

Searching for meaning

Rabbi/talmid relationship: a talmid (apprentice) walks in the rabbi's footsteps

Jesus' apprentice-disciples did learn concepts and beliefs but also shared emotions, attitudes, dispositions, behaviors, anxieties, uncertainties, hopes, and loyalties. All these were intertwined with certain smells, the taste of bread, and fish, the rocky road beneath the feet, the rocking of the boat, and the still quiet at night. Learning in this manner would reach more levels of character and consciousness than the linguistic mastery of contemporary schooling.

CHARLES F. MELCHERT, *WISE TEACHING*

DISCUSSION AND DEBATE 1

Small Groups: Consider using some or all of the following questions to provoke debate. (Do the same for the questions after DVD Segment 2.)

Individuals: If you're reading this on your own, try reflecting on some of these questions before continuing with the next section.

1. When Jesus first issued the challenge 'Follow me,' what did he mean? Do you think he meant it literally? When you chose to follow Jesus, was it just an internal decision, or did it involve taking action?

2. How does thinking of Jesus as a rabbi help your understanding of him as a teacher? How can the teaching styles of his culture affect how we learn from him today?

3. What's the difference between being a disciple and an apprentice? How does the word 'apprentice' affect your view of what it means to follow Jesus?

An ap·pren·tice is:

1: One who is learning by practical experience under skilled workers a trade, art or calling.

2: A beginner; a learner, an inexperienced person, a novice.

MERRIAM-WEBSTER'S COLLEGIATE DICTIONARY

4. How can we learn from practice, debate and mistakes? Is this way of learning more or less enriching than individual study?

5. Read Luke 5:4–11:

[Jesus] said to Simon, 'Now go out where it is deeper, and let down your nets to catch some fish.'

'Master,' Simon replied, 'we worked hard all last night and didn't catch a thing. But if you say so, I'll let the nets down again.' And this time their nets were so full of fish they began to tear!...

When Simon Peter realized what had happened, he fell to his knees before Jesus and said, 'Oh, Lord, please leave me — I'm too much of a sinner to be around you.'

... Jesus replied to Simon, 'Don't be afraid! From now on you'll be fishing for people!' And as soon as they landed, they left everything and followed Jesus. (NLT)

Do you think it's necessary to 'leave everything' to follow Jesus? What sacrifices have you made in order to follow his way?

Today, students want to know what their teacher knows so they can achieve a grade, complete a course or pass an exam. In contrast to this, a first-century apprentice wanted to be like their teacher – to become what the teacher was.

STEVE CHALKE, *APPRENTICE*

DVD SEGMENT 2

Watch the second video clip for this session, as people with differing perspectives and experiences of journeying, life and faith explore some of the issues raised by this section of *Apprentice*.

DVD Notes

DISCUSSION AND DEBATE 2

6. Do you think of life as a journey? If so, how does following Christ affect the direction of your journey?

7. Read Luke 9:57–60:

As they were walking along, someone said to Jesus, 'I will follow you wherever you go.'

But Jesus replied, 'Foxes have dens to live in, and birds have nests, but the Son of Man has no place even to lay his head.'

He said to another person, 'Come, follow me.'

The man agreed, but he said, 'Lord, first let me return home and bury my father.'

But Jesus told him, 'Let the spiritually dead bury their own dead! Your duty is to go and preach about the Kingdom of God.' (NLT)

What's the difference between *saying* you are a Christian and actively *following* Jesus?

8. Think about the idea that the Bible is a communal book. Can we fully understand its meaning by reading it on our own? How does discussing it with others affect how we learn?

9. Do you think we strengthen or weaken our sense of direction through a better understanding of other cultures and beliefs? For instance, how does a knowledge of Jewish culture deepen our understanding of what Jesus taught?

Apprentices trusted their rabbi completely, working passionately to incorporate his actions and attitudes, as well as his words, into their lives. A disciple's deepest desire was to follow his rabbi so closely that he would start to think, and act, just like him.

STEVE CHALKE, *APPRENTICE*

WRAP-UP (PRAYER IDEAS)

Pray that on your own journey you'll follow Jesus as his apprentice, even when that means making sacrifices.

Pray, too, for your group, church or community, that *together* you'll travel towards the truth, learning from each other and from your own experiences.

BETWEEN SESSIONS

See the 'Walk This Way' section, pages 14–16, for activities to help you grow as Jesus' apprentice between now and session two.

Walk This Way

Consider choosing one (or more) of the following suggested activities/ideas to reflect on prior to session two. Try to be as honest as possible in sharing with your friends or small group members any impact these choices have on you.

1. Read *Apprentice* chapter one—*Journeying*.

   Think about your everyday actions, in your home or workplace. How much do they reflect your desire to follow Jesus?

   How can you practically live out your decision to walk his way through life?

   Consider keeping a journal throughout the week, exploring how you can translate the desire to follow Jesus into reality during your daily life.

2. If you read the Bible during the week, note any passages that you find interesting and any questions the text raises. Make a point of discussing those passages and questions with your family, friends, small group or church members. Try to start thinking about the Bible as a *communal* book.

3. If possible, try reading a passage from the Bible out loud with friends, family or someone from your community, and then discussing it together. For instance, read Matthew 16:24–25:

   If any of you want to be my followers, you must forget about yourself. You must take up your cross and follow me. If you want to save your life, you will destroy it. But if you give up your life for me, you will find it. (CEV)

   Ensure that all those present feel encouraged to explore and debate the passage's meaning.

4. The Torah comprises the first five books of the Bible (also known as the Pentateuch), namely: Genesis, Exodus, Leviticus, Numbers and Deuteronomy. Jesus lived in a culture which communicated through word of mouth. The Torah was very often told from memory and then discussed. Try memorising a passage from the Bible and, if possible, recite it to a friend or family member, exploring with them what it might mean.

   Here's a passage from the Torah you could consider memorising:

   Moses replied, 'I have never been a good speaker. I wasn't one before you spoke to me, and I'm not one now. I am slow at speaking, and I can never think of what to say.'

   But the LORD answered, 'Who makes people able to speak or makes them deaf or unable to speak? Who gives them sight or makes them blind? Don't you know that I am the one who does these things? Now go! When you speak, I will be with you and give you the words to say.'

Exodus 4:10–12 CEV

In what way has memorising and discussing the text affected how you think about it?

Cheer up! On your feet! He's calling you.

Mark 10:49 NIV

RECOMMENDED RESOURCES FOR FURTHER READING

Abbot Christopher Jamison, *Finding Sanctuary: Monastic Steps for Everyday Life* (Phoenix, 2006)

Charles F. Melchert, *Wise Teaching* (Trinity Press International, 1998)

N. T. Wright, *Following Jesus: Biblical Reflections on Discipleship* (SPCK, 1994)

2

LONGING

My soul craves, but for what I don't know.

Erwin Raphael McManus, *Soul Cravings*

DVD SEGMENT 1

Watch the first video clip for session two, in which Steve Chalke tells the story of a man longing to leave home for a beautiful, faraway planet, before discussing consumerism, advertising and ownership. He then describes how Jesus viewed his own work—God's work—as sustaining, and how he believes that aligning our longings with the longings of God is the path to fulfilment.

DVD Notes

Edward Bernays, nephew of Freud: advertising linked to desire

Consumerism: more pleasure from acquiring than from owning

Jesus said: 'My food is to do the work of him who sent me' (John 4:34)

Aligning our longings with the longings of God

'Pray unceasingly' (1 Thessalonians 5:17)

Living out the Lord's Prayer

The truth is that our finest moments are most likely to occur when we are feeling deeply uncomfortable, unhappy, or unfulfilled. For it is only in such moments, propelled by our discomfort, that we are likely to step out of our ruts and start searching for different ways or truer answers.

M. SCOTT PECK, *THE ROAD LESS TRAVELLED*

DISCUSSION AND DEBATE 1

Small Groups: Consider using some or all of the following questions to provoke debate. (Do the same for the questions after DVD Segment 2.)

Individuals: If you're reading this on your own, try reflecting on some of these questions before continuing with the next section.

1. Do you generally find life more fulfilling or exhausting? Is your work, or lack of it, draining? What do you long to be different?

2. In John 6:27 (WE) Jesus says: *'Do not work for the food that spoils, but work for the food that will never spoil, the food that will give you life forever.'* To what extent do you feel trapped working for 'food that spoils'? Do you long for something deeper and more sustaining?

3. Does following Jesus change how we view our life's work? What is the relationship between your employment, or lack of it, and your life's work?

4. What kind of work did Jesus do, and why was it sustaining? Think of some examples of the kind of work we're called to do as Christ's apprentices.

5. In 1 Thessalonians 5:17 Paul urges us to 'pray continually'. How might a deep, spiritual longing enable us to do this?

6. Do you think some or any of your longings are aligned with the longings of God? Discuss how you can discover more about what God wants.

7. How can God's will be done 'on earth as it is in heaven'? Is this his responsibility or ours?

The longing for God that consumes the soul is true for all times. It cannot be otherwise when it comes from God himself. It must be forever. It has practically nothing to do with an emotional surge or single dedication of the heart to God's Word. It is a decision made for all time.

DIETRICH BONHOEFFER, *MEDITATIONS ON PSALMS* (PSALM 119)

DVD SEGMENT 2

Watch the second video clip for this session, as people with different experiences and expectations of life discuss their own longings, both spiritual and material.

DVD Notes

We are so easily led to purchase a product because a television or radio advertisement pronounces it better than any others. Advertisers have long since learned that most people are softminded, and they capitalize on this susceptibility ...

MARTIN LUTHER KING JR, *STRENGTH TO LOVE*

DISCUSSION AND DEBATE 2

8. What do you personally long for in life? What are your goals, your ambitions? Is it wrong to strive for the things you want?

9. We live in a consumerist society. What are the material things you crave? Think about how advertising has affected your answer. Is it wrong to strive for the material things you want?

10. How do you tell the difference between necessity and materialism? What's the difference between what you *need* and what you *want*?

11. Do you ever long for the impossible? Is what you crave out of reach? If so, is that part of the attraction?

12. If you gain what you crave, does it always fulfil you? If so, for how long? How soon do you start wanting something else? Think about whether the process of acquiring something, or the actual ownership itself, is more enjoyable — be as honest as you can.

13. Read the following verses:

You listen to the longings of those who suffer. You offer them hope, and you pay attention to their cries for help.

Psalm 10:17 CEV

All my longings lie open before you, O Lord; my sighing is not hidden from you.

Psalm 38:9 NIV

What do these texts tell us about God's understanding of our longings?

My soul is consumed with longing for your rules at all times.

Psalm 119:20 ESV

«« WRAP-UP (PRAYER IDEAS) »»

Pray that you will be able to further align your own longings with the longings of God, putting his will into action. Pray for your community, that it might look outwards not inwards, beyond its own needs to the needs of others.

Be silent for a few moments, offering your longings to God – without necessarily using words. Ask that the feeling of longing for God might infiltrate your everyday life so that you can 'pray continually'.

BETWEEN SESSIONS

See the 'Walk This Way' section, pages 27–33, for activities to help you grow as Jesus' apprentice between now and session three.

Walk This Way

Consider choosing one (or more) of the following suggested activities/ideas to reflect on prior to session three. Try to be as honest as possible in sharing with your friends or small group members any impact that these choices have on you.

1. Make a list of everything you buy during the week.

Every time you see advertising, think about how it affects your sense of longing and consumer choices. Do you really need all the things you buy?

Then think about the wider impact your purchases might have. Ask yourself whether you could make different choices.

How do your consumer choices affect others? For instance, do you choose Fairtrade and ethical products where possible, or do you buy the cheapest – or most expensive – option available? Are you attracted to particular brands or logos, and if so, why? What are the principles that guide you?

Weigh up your priorities and think about what you might do differently next week.

If our longings are channelled into the kind of work Jesus was talking about, our desires no longer drain us – they sustain us.

STEVE CHALKE, *APPRENTICE*

2. Read *Apprentice* chapter two – *Longing.* Write down your personal longings — the things you most want in life. Then write down, as far as you feel able, what you think God wants for you. Compare the two lists. How compatible are they?

MY LONGINGS	GOD'S LONGINGS FOR ME

Try to articulate your longings to God and/or, if possible, confide them to a trusted friend. How does expressing your longings make you feel?

Reflect on how you would feel if God's will were done on earth, here and now. Would that satisfy your own longings? If not, why not?

Think about your priorities and whether you could align them more closely with God's.

3. Think about the relationship between prayer and longing. Do you view prayer as an activity separate/apart from your everyday life? Do you find prayer difficult, or often feel you have 'run out of time' for prayer? If so, reflect on the following questions:

   • Have your prayers become formulaic?

   • Do you always use words?

   • Do your prayers express your deep longings, or have they become a matter of formality and habit?

   • Is it always necessary to have a daily allocated time for prayer, away from the realities of life?

- Has prayer become stressful, as though it's another 'task' to be completed?

- Are there patterns or habits of prayer which are helpful and liberating?

Consider how a real, constant longing to do God's will becomes the *continuous prayer* written about by Paul to the Thessalonians.

If necessary, stop putting pressure on yourself to conform to a particular pattern of prayer.

Try praying without words, during your everyday life, offering God your longing for him and for his will to be done.

Reflect on the following quote by Cardinal Basil Hume from his book *The Mystery of Love*. Try 'stealing moments out of the day' to 'explore God':

Meditation is what we do when we steal moments out of the day to be alone with God, however short that time may be; when we wonder what he is like, when we 'explore' God. But we need something to guide us in our exploration. There can be no better starting point than a passage from the Gospels, reading it slowly until it gives up its meaning; then it stirs your heart. When you start to meditate, you will find distractions galore, even boredom, the sense of getting nowhere. The point is you have to stick at it. You have to make an act of faith, because the moments you spend trying to raise your mind to God are precious and golden.

4. Think about Steve Chalke's story of the rabbi who helped the old woman each week (DVD Segment 1). Are there people in your own life whom you might be able to help in a practical way? Think realistically about whether you could fit this into your schedule.

Are you realistically able to offer any more time (even in a small way) to someone else, such as a friend, family member, a member of your church or wider community?

Think globally: what are the situations world-wide that concern you, and are there ways you can help?

Then weigh up your own needs and longings. Where do they fit into this picture? Do you have enough time for yourself? When in life might you take the role of the rabbi in the story, and when might you be the person in need? Are you open to accept help when it is offered, as well as offering it to others?

Read 2 Timothy 3:10–17:

You've been a good apprentice to me, a part of my teaching, my manner of life, direction, faith, steadiness, love, patience, troubles, sufferings ...

... Stick with what you learned and believed, sure of the integrity of your teachers ... Through the Word we are put together and shaped up for the tasks God has for us. (The Message)

Think about Paul and Timothy and how they relate to each other. When are you called to be more like Paul – offering help and encouragement – and when, like Timothy, do you need to receive support or advice?

5. Discipline is frequently seen as the enemy of freedom. We often assume that the fulfilment of our longings comes from a removal or lack of boundaries. But think about the girl who longs to be a famous musician. Only by practising regularly can she achieve her goal.

   Look again at the lists you made of your own longings, and God's longings for you. Could an increased sense of discipline or structure bring any of these desires to fruition? What practical changes to your daily life might help transform those positive longings into action?

Monastic communities live by a 'rule' (meaning 'measure'). This is often misunderstood as a harsh set of restrictions, but in fact a 'rule' of this kind is a liberating routine that makes time for God and others. People who live by a simple rule invariably find the sense of order and discipline it brings liberating, not limiting. (For more on rules of life, read *Apprentice* chapter nine – *Listening*.)

Think about your own routine. Are there simple ways you could inject more discipline into your life in a way that would be freeing?

Plan a week that incorporates small amounts of time for activities that reflect Christ's own pattern of living, such as specific moments of prayer, reflecting on the words of the Bible, acts of service or spending time with your family, friends or community.

Don't be unrealistic—if you set yourself impossible tasks, nothing will change. Think about what you can manage, and over the coming weeks try to put your own personal 'rule' into practice. Reflect on how your altered routine makes you feel, and report back to your small group.

God intends the disciplines of the spiritual life to be for ordinary human beings: people who have jobs, who care for children, who must wash dishes and mow lawns. In fact, the Disciplines are best exercised in the midst of our normal activities. If they are to have a transforming effect, the effect must be found in the ordinary junctures of human life.

RICHARD FOSTER, *CELEBRATION OF DISCIPLINE*

RECOMMENDED RESOURCES FOR FURTHER READING

Esther de Waal, *A Life-Giving Way: A Commentary on the Rule of St. Benedict* (Liturgical Press, 1995)

Richard Foster, *Celebration of Discipline* (Hodder, 1978)

Abbot Christopher Jamison, *Finding Happiness: Monastic Steps for a Fulfilling Life* (Weidenfeld & Nicolson, 2008)

Erwin Raphael McManus, *Soul Cravings* (Nelson Books, 2006)

M. Scott Peck, *The Road Less Travelled* (Arrow, 1990)

Ronald Rolheiser, *Against an Infinite Horizon* (Hodder and Stoughton, 1995)

3

BELIEVING

When he was raised from death, his disciples remembered what he had told them. Then they believed the Scriptures and the words of Jesus.

John 2:22 CEV

DVD SEGMENT 1

Watch the first video clip for session three, in which Steve Chalke begins with the story of a lost man trying to journey on the London Underground before describing meeting a group of teenagers who have questions about faith and God. He then discusses the difference between intellectual belief and dynamic, risk-taking faith. This section concludes with a story about two apprentices: one cynical, one prepared to be patient. Steve explores the idea that it is only as we take time to look for God that we can find him.

DVD Notes

We all live by faith, whether or not we believe in God

What we have faith in needs to be worth it

Faith: believing something enough for it to change how you live

God is subtle

God meets us as we question and reflect

DISCUSSION AND DEBATE 1

Small Groups: Consider using some or all of the following questions to provoke debate. (Do the same for the questions after DVD Segment 2.)

Individuals: If you're reading this on your own, try reflecting on some of these questions before continuing with the next section.

1. Is what you put your faith in worth it? Has your faith changed the way you live?

2. Read Proverbs 14:15:

    A simple man believes anything, but a prudent man gives thought to his steps. (NIV)

    How can we avoid simply believing everything we're told? How do we determine what to believe?

3. Think about the following interrelated ideas, debating which explanations you find most convincing:

    *   If someone doesn't believe in God, this is either an *absence* of faith, or an *expression* of faith.

    *   An agnostic is either someone who lacks the gift of faith, *or*

someone who invests their faith in our inability to find the truth.

- Consider whether 'facts' can really be proven, or whether we need to have faith to believe they are true.

4. Science and religion are often seen as mutually exclusive – you have to believe in one or the other. But how might they complement each other? How might they conflict?

Science investigates; religion interprets. Science gives man knowledge which is power; religion gives man wisdom which is control. Science deals mainly with facts; religion deals mainly with values. The two are not rivals. They are complementary.

MARTIN LUTHER KING JR, *STRENGTH TO LOVE*

5. Read Isaiah 43:3–7:

I am the LORD, your God, the Holy One of Israel, the God who saves you ... To me, you are very dear, and I love you. That's why I gave up nations and people to rescue you. Don't be afraid! I am with you. From both east and west, I will bring you together. I will say to the north and to the south, 'Free my sons and daughters! Let them return from distant lands. They are my people – I created each of them to bring honor to me.' (CEV)

How does this text illuminate your conception of God? Focus especially on the words *'To me, you are very dear, and I love you … Don't be afraid! I am with you.'*

Discuss the idea that God is subtle and gentle. Does this fit with your current idea of God? Why is God so often portrayed as stern and disapproving?

6. Discuss the story of the prodigal son in Luke 15:11 – 31. The father welcomes his son without recriminations, despite the son's faults and failings. Do you believe God loves you unconditionally? Do you ever struggle with this idea? If so, why?

We run from God because we long to be loved and we have convinced ourselves that the One who is most loving could not and would not embrace us.

ERWIN RAPHAEL MCMANUS, *SOUL CRAVINGS*

DVD SEGMENT 2

Watch the second video clip for this session, as people with differing perspectives and experiences of faith explore some of the issues raised by this section of *Apprentice*.

DVD Notes

DISCUSSION AND DEBATE 2

7. Does believing in God ever make you feel stupid? Explain.

8. Are *faith* and *certainty* the same thing? Is *belief* the same as *knowledge*?

Are you more comfortable assenting to beliefs in your head, or embracing them with your heart? Why?

9. Do you think healthy Christian spirituality can be expressed in 'black and white' terms, or, in your view, does faith come in shades of grey?

Be as honest as you can about your own journey – whether you think it's more well-defined and bounded, or more fluid, dynamic or mysterious.

10. How is having faith the same as taking a risk? In your own life, has following Jesus involved taking risks?

◀◀ WRAP-UP (PRAYER IDEAS) ▶▶

Pray that you will be able to place your trust in God as you progress on life's journey.

Pray for a dynamic, risk-taking faith: a faith that moves beyond a set of beliefs in your head to a new way of living and walking with Jesus – even when that journey takes you in unexpected directions.

BETWEEN SESSIONS

See the 'Walk This Way' section, pages 42–46, for activities to help you grow as Jesus' apprentice between now and session four.

Walk This Way

Consider choosing one (or more) of the following suggested activities/ideas to reflect on prior to session four. Try to be as honest as possible in sharing with your friends or small group members any impact that these choices have on you.

1. Write down what you feel to be the main influences in your life, the things in which you place your trust. Examples might include:

Family	Culture/society	Science
Friends	Status	Education
God	Wealth	Health
Church	Appearance	Government/ democracy
Community	Media	Justice system

Then rate how much faith you put in each one, on a scale of 1 to 10 (1 would represent a very small investment of faith, 10 would represent a certainty of belief). Be as honest as you can.

Do your answers surprise you?

Which factors in your life turn out to be the most influential? Which do you place the most faith in?

Ask yourself whether the people, ideas or institutions which influence you most are reliable or worthwhile. You may be happy with your choices. But if not, who or what would you like to place more faith in? Is anything holding you back?

Everyone who does believe him has shown that God is truthful. The Son was sent to speak God's message, and he has been given the full power of God's Spirit.

John 3:33–34 CEV

2. Read *Apprentice* chapter three–*Believing*. Then reflect on what it is you believe. Make a list of some of the key aspects of your faith–the values you hold most dear.

Look over your list. Did you struggle to put into words what it is you value about your faith? Are you most comfortable with rules and certainties, or did you find your spirituality difficult to define?

Think about the idea that faith is dynamic, active and alive. Does your faith feel alive? Has it changed any aspects of how you try to live your life?

Consider how your beliefs might be lived out. Try to start thinking of yourself as an apprentice. The apprentices of Jesus learned through experiences – both successes and mistakes. Their beliefs were formed organically. They didn't swallow a set of ideas without experimenting with and questioning them first. How similar or different is this from your own experiences?

Over the coming week, remember that you are Christ's apprentice. Keep a brief journal about how this makes you feel – does it make your faith feel more or less alive? Does it make any difference to how you live each day?

3. Research some of the different portrayals of God in the media. Keep your eyes open for references to God or Christianity in newspapers, on the TV, advertising, the Internet and so on. Note down any key themes which emerge.

How is God generally viewed? Does this vary widely depending on who describes him?

Note the differences in how God is portrayed by:

- Christians of different persuasions
- Atheists
- Agnostics
- Other faith groups

Think about your own view of God. Ask yourself to what extent this has been shaped by the media, family, friends and other influences.

Read Psalm 107, which emphasises that God's *love endures forever* and often repeats the phrase *and he saved them from their distress*.

How accurate or misleading are different Christian portrayals of God? How accurate or misleading are different media portrayals of God?

Are you used to thinking of God as loving you unconditionally, or do you worry about how God views you?

Try to find a loving image of a parent embracing or watching over their child. Look at it for a while. What does it tell you about God's attitude towards us?

Meditate on the God who loves you.

If we believe in the God who raised Jesus, then, as our fears are dealt with at a deeper and deeper level, as they are met by the astonishing love of the surpassing God, we will be able to leave behind the image of a bossy, bullying God who wants to keep his laws in order to control us, to lick us into shape, to squash or stifle our humanness or our individuality. Instead, we will be able to follow the true God, the God who raises the dead, in trust rather than fear.

N. T. WRIGHT, *FOLLOWING JESUS*

RECOMMENDED RESOURCES FOR FURTHER READING

Martin Luther King, Jr, *Strength to Love* (Augsburg Fortress, 1981 edition)

Brennan Manning, *Ruthless Trust* (SPCK, 1992)

Philip Yancey, *What's So Amazing About Grace?* (Zondervan, 1997)

4

BELONGING

Loneliness and the feeling of being unwanted is the most terrible poverty.

Mother Teresa

DVD SEGMENT 1

Watch the first video clip for session four, in which Steve starts with a story contrasting the professor who learns the academic theory of love and a young woman whose love for her child is instinctive. Steve then goes on to discuss the Trinity, our model for the meaning of love and its implications for the diversity of healthy community. He closes by emphasising the central teachings of Jesus: love God, love others, love yourself.

DVD Notes

We can't love in a vacuum

God *is* love

The Trinity is a diverse community

We are made in God's image—so we are made for community

The main principles of Jesus: Love God, love others as you love yourself. Nothing else matters.

Since God is a Trinity—a community—this brings new depth to our understanding of what it means for humans to be made in the image of God. It means that we only ever realise our full potential as human beings in community with God and with others.

STEVE CHALKE, *APPRENTICE*

DISCUSSION AND DEBATE 1

Small Groups: Consider using some or all of the following questions to provoke debate. (Do the same for the questions after DVD Segment 2.)

Individuals: If you're reading this on your own, try reflecting on some of these questions before continuing with the next section.

1. Think about the story of the professor and the mother. Who do you honestly most identify with? Are you more comfortable with the *concept* of unconditional love or with the *reality* of it?

2. Read Mark 2:14–17:

   As he walked along, [Jesus] saw Levi son of Alphaeus sitting at the tax collector's booth. 'Follow me,' Jesus told him, and Levi got up and followed him.

   While Jesus was having dinner at Levi's house, many tax collectors and 'sinners' were eating with him and his disciples, for there were many who followed him. When the teachers of the law who were Pharisees saw him eating with the 'sinners' and tax collectors, they asked his disciples: 'Why does he eat with tax collectors and "sinners"?'

   On hearing this, Jesus said to them, 'It is not the healthy who need a doctor, but the sick. I have not come to call the righteous, but sinners.' (NIV)

   What does this passage tell us about Jesus' attitude towards inclusion and diversity? Is his attitude reflected in your own church or community?

3. Read Philippians 2:1–5:

   Christ encourages you, and his love comforts you. God's Spirit unites you, and you are concerned for others. Now make me completely happy! Live in harmony by showing love for each other. Be united in what you think, as if you were only one person. Don't be jealous or proud, but be humble and consider others more important than yourselves. Care about them as much as you care about yourselves and think the same way that Christ Jesus thought. (CEV)

   Paul calls for unity amongst communities. Bearing in mind the nature of the Trinity, discuss the idea that healthy communities should be both unified *and* diverse. Is this possible? How?

4. Discuss why loneliness has become so prevalent in our world. Why do communities break down? Do we expect too much of our communities, or not enough?

5. In Matthew 22:37–40 (CEV) Jesus says: *"'Love the Lord your God with all your heart, soul, and mind." This is the first and most important commandment. The second most important commandment is like this one. And it is, "Love others as much as you love yourself." All the Law of Moses and the Books of the*

Prophets are based on these two commandments.' How do you think Jesus' two main principles – love God, love others as yourself – are related? Is one or other of these principles usually easier or more challenging to live out?

He who loves his dream of a community more than the community itself becomes a destroyer of the latter, even though his personal intentions may be ever so honest and earnest and sacrificial.

DIETRICH BONHOEFFER, *LIFE TOGETHER*

DVD SEGMENT 2

Watch the second video clip for this session, which features reflections on belonging from a cross-section of individuals with different experiences of community.

DVD Notes

Loneliness is one of the most universal sources of human suffering today … Children, adolescents, adults, and old people are in growing degree exposed to the contagious disease of loneliness.

HENRI NOUWEN, *REACHING OUT*

DISCUSSION AND DEBATE 2

6. How important is it to you that you 'belong'? Does this sense of belonging/wanting to belong change depending on who you're with? If so, why is this?

7. Read Acts 2:44–46:

All the Lord's followers often met together, and they shared everything they had. They would sell their property and posses-sions and give the money to whoever needed it. Day after day they met together in the temple. They broke bread together in different homes and shared their food happily and freely. (CEV)

Discuss what this passage tells us about early Christian com-munities. Is this reflected by your church community, or by any churches/communities that you know of? If not, why not?

What are the important principles from the church in Acts 2 that we can apply to our lives and society?

8. What are some of the challenges that community brings? What are some of the benefits?

9. Read James 2:1–4, 8–9:

   My friends, if you have faith in our glorious Lord Jesus Christ, you won't treat some people better than others. Suppose a rich person wearing fancy clothes and a gold ring comes to one of your meetings. And suppose a poor person dressed in worn-out clothes also comes. You must not give the best seat to the one in fancy clothes and tell the one who is poor to stand at the side or sit on the floor. That is the same as saying that some people are better than others …

   You will do all right, if you obey the most important law in the Scriptures. It is the law that commands us to love others as much as we love ourselves. But if you treat some people better than others, you have done wrong … (CEV)

   James warns against favouritism and excluding the poor. In your own church or community, are there cliques or social hierarchies? Is it really possible to 'love your neighbour' with equality and fairness? What would this mean in practical terms?

10. If community life doesn't live up to our ideals, is it worth it? Why do we bother interacting with others when they might hurt us?

11. Do you ever feel lonely even when you're with other people? Discuss the idea that overcoming loneliness isn't just about being with others, but is about connecting with them. How can we facilitate this?

There is no safe investment. To love at all is to be vulnerable.

C. S. LEWIS, *THE FOUR LOVES*

◀◀ WRAP-UP (PRAYER IDEAS) ▶▶

Pray that everyone in your church would experience being part of an integrated, vibrant community, where people can really be themselves.

Pray that visitors and newcomers to your church community feel welcome–rather than overwhelmed, excluded or intimidated.

Remember, too, all who are lonely, whether through isolation, or from a lack of close relationships.

BETWEEN SESSIONS

See the 'Walk This Way' section, pages 57–61, for activities to help you grow as Jesus' apprentice between now and session five.

Walk This Way

Consider choosing one (or more) of the following suggested activities/ideas to reflect on prior to session five. Try to be as honest as possible in sharing with your friends or small group members any impact that these choices have on you.

1. Think about whether you feel you belong to different groups or communities. Consider writing down any different groups you are in any way involved with. Examples could include:

Family	Clubs/societies
Church	Parenting groups
School/college/university	Internet groups/communities
Work	Union
Sports team	Committee
Band/orchestra	Other friendship groups

Then evaluate which, if any, of these groups make you feel truly welcome. Do you feel you can really be yourself in any of these groups? Or do you have to significantly change or adapt your behaviour in order to 'fit in'?

Perhaps you don't feel you belong in any particular group. What is it that makes you feel isolated or unwelcome? Do you think this is the fault of others? Are there healthier communities you could consider getting involved with?

Reflect on which group(s) or communities might be really worth your investment of time and energy, and whether others are less worthwhile.

Consider which relationships you might want to develop more, and how you could practically put your energies into nurturing these fruitfully.

2. Many communities rely on a small group of people to do the majority of the organisation of their community life. It may be that some of these people genuinely have more time to give. But there may also be others who are becoming over-stretched by their involvement. Think about your own role in your church community. Are you usually one of the people involved with much of the community's work? If so, do you ever feel so over-burdened with tasks that you end up finding belonging more stifling than fulfilling? Think about whether you might be able to delegate some of your tasks so that you have more opportunity to enjoy the benefits of community. If you feel trapped by your

duties, consider whether there is someone–perhaps a leader or wise friend–in whom you could confide who might be able to help free you from this sense of obligation.

On the other hand, are you someone who generally relies on others to organise the running of your community? Realistically, are there ways you might be able to offer even a small amount of time to contribute more to the life of your community? Even if your time is severely limited, could you, for instance, engage a visitor in conversation, call someone who lives alone, or pick up some shopping for someone while you do your own? Think of practical ways you can enrich community life without becoming over-burdened yourself.

Then think about the value of devoting time to yourself, time away from community. In your own life, is there a balance between getting involved and having time for yourself? If not, what would you like to change, and how might this be achieved?

3. Read *Apprentice* chapter five–*Belonging*. Write down a list of qualities that your ideal community might have. Then list what characterises the reality of life in your community–both its strengths and weaknesses.

What are the differences/similarities between your ideal and the reality?

For many of us, there's likely to be a significant gap between our ideals and our actual experience of community. Why do you think this is?

Do you think we expect too much of community life, or do you think we neglect ways to improve it?

Reflect on the idea that although communities are flawed, they can still be enriching. Does this alter your perspective, the way you think of your own community?

How good and pleasant it is when brothers live together in unity!

Psalm 133:1 NIV

4. For our Christian faith to be authentic, we need to be with God for other people, and with other people for God. In many ways, finding a balanced role in our communities is about finding an equilibrium between 'intimacy' with God (through the development of a living and honest relationship with him) and 'involvement' with others (the natural outflow of that relationship into all other areas of life). In the teaching of Jesus, intimacy and involvement are always organically connected. The combination

is vital. (For more on intimacy and involvement, read *Apprentice* chapter ten–*Engaging*).

Think about the inter-connected ideas of intimacy and involvement. In your own life, is there a balance between the two? Do you feel your faith combines your relationship with God and your relationships with others in a way that's effective?

Reflect on whether you might be more comfortable nurturing intimacy with God than engaging with others. Alternatively, you might be at home with involvement and activism, living out the practical dimensions of your faith, but feel you are missing the opportunity or inner longing to nurture a more intimate relationship with God.

How can you find practical ways of further integrating these two aspects of your faith?

Note any ideas about how intimacy and involvement relate to each other in your life, and bring your thoughts to your next small group discussion.

RECOMMENDED RESOURCES FOR FURTHER READING

Dietrich Bonhoeffer, *Life Together: The Classic Exploration of Faith in Community* (HarperOne, 1978)

Steve Chalke and Simon Johnston, *Intimacy and Involvement* (Kingsway, 2003)

Shane Claiborne, *The Irresistible Revolution: Living as an Ordinary Radical* (Zondervan, 2007)

Henri Nouwen, *Reaching Out* (Zondervan, 1998)

5

QUESTIONING

If only God would give me some clear sign! Like
making a large deposit in my name at a Swiss bank.

Woody Allen

DVD SEGMENT 1

Watch the first video clip for session five, in which Steve Chalke explores
the idea that questioning is not only natural; it is also a crucial tool for
examining, testing and strengthening faith. Questions are not to be
feared; instead, we should be worried when people don't have questions, or don't feel free to raise them.

As Christ's apprentices, we have the opportunity and, at the same time,
the responsibility to question and debate in the context of community.

Not to do so creates a barrier to honesty and blocks development. Only through probing our faith are we able to journey towards maturity and understanding.

The power to question is the basis of all human progress.

INDIRA GANDHI

DVD Notes

Expect the unexpected

Without room for doubt, faith could not exist

Jesus allowed his apprentices to explore their doubts

Thomas

Doubt isn't the opposite of faith; it's at the heart of it

If a man will begin with certainties, he shall end in doubts. But if he will be content to begin with doubts, he shall end in certainties.

PHILOSOPHER FRANCIS BACON

DISCUSSION AND DEBATE 1

Small Groups: Consider using some or all of the following questions to provoke debate. (Do the same for the questions after DVD Segment 2.)

Individuals: If you're reading this on your own, try reflecting on some of these questions before continuing with the next section.

1. Read John 20:24 – 28:

   Thomas (called Didymus), one of the Twelve, was not with the disciples when Jesus came. So the other disciples told him, 'We have seen the Lord!'

   But he said to them, 'Unless I see the nail marks in his hands and put my finger where the nails were, and put my hand into his side, I will not believe it.'

   A week later his disciples were in the house again, and Thomas was with them. Though the doors were locked, Jesus came and stood among them and said, 'Peace be with you!' Then he said to Thomas, 'Put your finger here; see my hands. Reach out your hand and put it into my side. Stop doubting and believe.'

   Thomas said to him, 'My Lord and my God!' (NIV)

Jesus creates the opportunity for Thomas to explore his doubts. As a direct outcome of this, the disciple history remembers as 'doubting Thomas' makes a more profound and articulate declaration of faith–*'My Lord and my God!'*–than any other apprentice of Christ had done until that moment. What does this encounter tell you about the attitude of Jesus towards our doubts and questions?

2. What are the biggest doubts and questions you have about your faith? If Jesus walked into the room, what would you really like to ask him? Be as honest as possible.

Sometimes I lie awake at night, and ask, 'Where have I gone wrong?' Then a voice says to me, 'This is going to take more than one night.'

CHARLES M. SCHULZ

3. Why do you think it is so commonly believed that doubt is dangerous? To what extent can doubt be a helpful way of examining what we believe and strengthening our faith?

Doubt is the instrument to purify my faith. It is only when I begin to doubt that I really make an honest act of faith.

CARDINAL BASIL HUME, *THE MYSTERY OF LOVE*

4. Discuss the pros and cons of the idea of 'unwavering' faith. Do you think this is desirable or healthy? Does this kind of faith even exist?

An inflexible faith risks not only stagnation, but, perhaps most damaging of all, complacency. Unless we are constantly examining what we stand for, what we hold to be precious and significant, and what, on the other hand, is mere paraphernalia tacked on to the real truth of the message Jesus taught, then we risk sinking into being too comfortable, too self-absorbed and too self-satisfied to live out an active faith at all.

STEVE CHALKE, *APPRENTICE*

DVD SEGMENT 2

Watch the second video clip for session five, as people with differing perspectives and experiences of life and faith explore some of the questions raised by this section of *Apprentice*.

What people don't realize is how much religion costs. They think faith is a big electric blanket, when of course it's a cross. It's much harder to believe than not to believe. If you feel you can't believe, you must at least do this: keep an open mind. Keep it open toward faith, keep wanting it, keep asking for it, and leave the rest to God.

FLANNERY O'CONNOR, *THE HABIT OF BEING*

DVD Notes

Everyone who is fully trained will be like his teacher.

Luke 6:40 NIV

DISCUSSION, DEBATE AND CONCLUSION

5. Do you think asking questions is more or less important than having answers? If we had all the answers, would we still actively engage with God?

6. How easy or difficult do you find it to make yourself vulnerable? Are you ever afraid that being honest about your questions will make you look stupid? If so, why?

7. Read the following verses:

Peter came up to the Lord and asked, 'How many times should I forgive someone who does something wrong to me? Is seven times enough?' Jesus answered: 'Not just seven times, but seventy-seven times!'

Matthew 18:21–22 CEV

Peter said, 'Explain the parable to us.'

Matthew 15:15 NIV

Peter was often asking questions–and making mistakes–yet Jesus entrusted him with great responsibility. How does asking questions equip us to follow Jesus?

An apprentice's deepest desire was to follow his rabbi so closely that he would start to think, and act, just like him. Many Jewish scholars believe that this offers the best understanding of how Peter briefly walked on water. When Jesus (the rabbi) was seen walking out on the lake, Peter (the talmid) felt the need to imitate his rabbi (see Matthew 14:22–33).

STEVE CHALKE, *APPRENTICE*

8. If you have completed all five *Apprentice* sessions, look back over the whole series. Are there any key questions, messages or insights which stand out for you?

9. Will *Apprentice* make any differences to the way you approach life, and faith, in the future?

All things are yours, . . . the world or life or death or the present or the future — all are yours, and you are of Christ, and Christ is of God.

1 Corinthians 3:21 – 23 NIV

❲❲ WRAP-UP (PRAYER IDEAS) ❳❳

Pray for an active, dynamic faith which allows space for you, and others, to question and engage with God.

Pray that through your example, commitment and honesty others will be liberated to voice their honest questions as they journey forward as apprentices of Jesus.

> *I pray that the Lord will listen when you are in trouble, and keep you safe.*
> *May the Lord send help and come to your rescue.*
> *May God give you the desires of your heart, and let all go well for you.*
> *May the Lord answer all of your prayers.*
> *We trust you, Lord God.*
>
> *(Based on Psalm 20)*

IN THE COMING DAYS

See the 'Walk This Way' section, pages 71 – 72, for activities to help you grow as Jesus' apprentice in the days and weeks ahead.

Walk This Way

Consider choosing one (or more) of the following suggested activities/ideas to reflect on in the coming days. Try to be as honest as possible in sharing with your friends or small group members any impact that these choices have on you.

1. Read *Apprentice* chapter four–*Questioning*. Think about any questions you may have about faith. Your questions might concern God's nature or existence, the relevance of Christian faith in today's world, the extent to which Christians reflect Jesus, ethical or moral dilemmas, or questions about yourself.

   Give yourself time to think through any persistent doubts or problems which may trouble you. Try offering these questions to God. Ask them openly and freely. If you feel anger or fear, express it. Imagine yourself in conversation with God. What is it you really want to say?

   Reflect on how engaging with God in this way makes you feel. Does it feel strange to question God? Is it unsettling? Is it liberating? Remember that God welcomes our questions and that addressing God in this honest way is an act of faith.

   Then about that time Jesus shouted, 'Eloi, Eloi, lema sabachthani?' which means, 'My God, my God, why have you deserted me?'

   Mark 15:34 CEV (quoting Psalm 22:1)

2. Try to find some passages in the Bible which involve questioning. Note any examples which particularly interest you. For example, you could look especially at:

   • Moses (especially in the book of Exodus)

   • The Psalms

- The book of Ecclesiastes
- The Gospels

The Bible is often presented as a book of certainties. Were you surprised at just how much questioning there is in the Bible, and how intensely it is expressed?

Bearing in mind your findings, what do you think the role of questioning is in the life of an apprentice of Jesus?

What does the level of questioning in the Bible tell you about God and about faith?

RECOMMENDED RESOURCES FOR FURTHER READING

K. J. Clark, *When Faith Is Not Enough* (W. B. Eerdmans, 1994)

Cardinal Basil Hume, *The Mystery of Love* (Darton, Longman and Todd, 2000 edition)

Henri J. M. Nouwen, *Show Me the Way* (Darton, Longman and Todd, 1993)

Philip Yancey, *Where Is God When It Hurts?* (Zondervan, 1990)

May God bless you with discomfort

at easy answers, half truths and superficial relationships

so that you may live deep within your heart.

May God bless you with anger

at injustice, oppression and exploitation of people

so that you may work for justice, freedom and peace.

May God bless you with tears

to shed for those who suffer pain, rejection, hunger and war

so that you may reach out your hand to comfort them and

to turn their pain into joy.

And may God bless you with enough foolishness

to believe that you can make a difference in the world

so that you can do what others claim cannot be done.

Amen.

Old Franciscan Blessing

Apprentice

Walking the Way of Christ

Steve Chalke with Joanna Wyld

The quest for meaning and purpose dwells within all of us. Jesus insisted that its fulfilment lay in a relationship with him. But what does that relationship look like—really?

Apprentice calls spiritual pilgrims, both Christians and non-Christians, to exchange the shallow diversions of secular and religious culture for the pursuit of our true desires. In a book of refreshing honesty, great heart, and rich creativity, Steve Chalke guides us into an apprenticeship with the master teacher, Jesus. Embarking on a relational journey that engages us on every level, we walk with Jesus through an organic, whole-life learning experience, exploring ten areas foundational to the meaning and depth we crave.

Apprentice encourages us to ask our most probing questions, embrace our doubts, and learn why we are driven to belong. Combining story and parable with thoughtful commentary, we discover the ancient art and discipline of apprenticeship—living lives stamped with the character, presence, and impact of Jesus.

Softcover 978-0-310-29154-1

The Lost Message of Jesus

Steve Chalke and Alan Mann

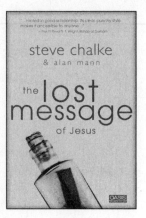

Who is the real Jesus? Do we remake him in our own image and then wonder why our spirituality is less than life-changing and exciting? Steve Chalke and Alan Mann believe that the real Jesus is deeply challenging. And each new generation must grapple with the question of who he is, because only through a constant study of Jesus are we able to discover God himself.

The Lost Message of Jesus is written to stir thoughtful debate and pose fresh questions that will help create a deeper understanding of Jesus and his message. It is an encounter with the real Jesus of his world—not the Jesus we try to mold to ours. Themes include:

- The Kingdom of God—shalom—is available to everyone now, through Jesus
- The world outside your own church needs to hear of the depth of God's love and suffering
- Jesus was a radical and a revolutionary!
- Jesus offers immediate forgiveness, without cost, to anyone

Focusing on some of the key episodes, events, and issues of Jesus' life, we will see how too often the message we preach today has been influenced more by the culture we live in than the radical, life-changing, world-shaping message Jesus shared two thousand years ago.

Softcover: 978-0-310-24882-8

Change Agents

25 Hard-Learned Lessons in the Art of Getting Things Done

Steve Chalke

Change agents are pioneers, entre-
preneurs, innovators. They can be difficult, annoying, and demanding. But
their calling is demanding too: to take a vision and wrench it
into reality.

When Steve Chalke was asked to be the senior minister of
a dying inner-city church, he knew what he wanted: to make
it into a Christian equivalent of a first-century synagogue. A
place where the community gathered, not just to pray and hear
sermons, but to be educated, entertained, and to find help.

Making it all happen was the harder part. In *Change Agents*,
the author shares twenty-five lessons he learned during this
work. He had to teach himself to respond, not react; say no
more than yes, give up being everyone's friend, and accept that
any success was only a short respite between two crises.

Employing wry humour, personal examples, and a large
helping of practical advice, Steve Chalke reminds us that our
enterprise, not our caution, with the Word of God is what's
rewarded. Christ waits and watches for us to take risks and
create change in the church, the community and the world
at large.

Softcover: 978-0-310-27549-7

Intelligent Church

A Journey Towards Christ-Centred Community

Steve Chalke with Anthony Watkis

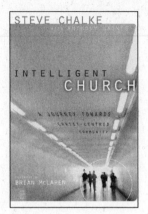

'Everything that Steve Chalke writes is insightful and cutting-edge. Here he argues in favour of a church that thinks and acts in ways that make the Kingdom of God visible and reasonable in a secular society.'

– Tony Campolo, PhD
Eastern University, Pennsylvania, USA

The task of the Church is 'to be the irrefutable demonstration and proof of the fact that God is love,' claims Steve Chalke. An intelligent church intentionally connects the Bible and its twenty-first-century culture, is authentic and, most importantly, has thought through its practice. In other words, the way it does church is a reflection of its understanding of who God is.

This foundational issue must be addressed by pastors, church and ministry leaders, small group leaders and others as we continue to grapple with the shape of effective church in the postmodern, post-Christian West.

As Chalke unpacks central theological concepts, such as the incarnation, human sinfulness, and the Trinity, he points us to the corresponding characteristics of an intelligent church, such as inclusiveness, messiness and diversity. Each thought-provoking chapter concludes with a 'Yes but How?' section, which gives practical suggestions for moving your church along this path.

Softcover: 978-0-310-24884-2

Share Your Thoughts

With the Author: Your comments will be forwarded to
the author when you send them to *zauthor@zondervan.com*.

With Zondervan: Submit your review of this book
by writing to *zreview@zondervan.com*.

Free Online Resources at
www.zondervan.com

Zondervan AuthorTracker: Be notified whenever your
favorite authors publish new books, go on tour, or post
an update about what's happening in their lives.

Daily Bible Verses and Devotions: Enrich your life
with daily Bible verses or devotions that help you start
every morning focused on God.

Free Email Publications: Sign up for newsletters on
fiction, Christian living, church ministry, parenting, and
more.

Zondervan Bible Search: Find and compare
Bible passages in a variety of translations at
www.zondervanbiblesearch.com.

Other Benefits: Register yourself to receive online
benefits like coupons and special offers, or to participate
in research.